Captain Cook

Oxford University Press, 198 Madison Avenue, New York NY 10016

Oxford New York
Athens Auckland Bangkok Bogotá Buenos Aires
Calcutta Cape Town Chennai Dar es Salaam Delhi
Florence Hong Kong Istanbul Karachi Kuala Lumpur
Madrid Melbourne Mexico City Mumbai
Nairobi Paris São Paulo Singapore
Taipei Tokyo Toronto Warsaw

and associated companies in
Berlin Ibadan

Oxford is a trademark of Oxford University Press

Text © Andrew Langley 1997
Illustrations © Oxford University Press 1997
Published by Oxford University Press, NY, 1998
Originally published by Oxford University Press UK in 1997

Library of Congress Cataloging-in-Publication Data

Middleton, Haydn.
    Captain Cook: the great ocean explorer / Haydn Middleton;
illustrated by Alan Marks.
        p.   cm.—(What's their story?)
    Includes index.
        1. Cook, James, 1728–1779—Juvenile literature.   2. Explorers—
Great Britain—Biography—Juvenile literature.   [1. Cook, James,
1728–1779.   2. Explorers.]   I. Marks, Alan, 1957–   ill.   II. Title.
III. Series.
G246.C7M43   1998
910'.92—dc21
[B]   97–42081
                                                                              CIP
                                                                              AC

1 3 5 7 9 10 8 6 4 2

ISBN 0-19-521433-1 (hardback)

Printed in Dubai by Oriental Press

Captain Cook

THE GREAT OCEAN EXPLORER

HAYDN MIDDLETON

Illustrated by Alan Marks

OXFORD UNIVERSITY PRESS

James Cook was born in 1728, in the village of Marton in the north of England. His family did farm work, and they lived in a small cottage with earthen walls on the edge of the Yorkshire moors.

As James grew up, he helped on the farm. But he also learned to read and write and became very good at arithmetic. When he had any free time, he went down to the coast to watch the ships passing by. They were carrying coal down to London, where King George II had his court.

James loved to gaze out to sea. His secret dream was to be a sailor. He longed to visit London, and cities in foreign countries as well. Perhaps he might even travel on a ship to lands that nobody yet knew about.

At the age of 17, James got a job. He became a shop clerk in the nearby village of Staithes, selling groceries and sewing materials.

This was a good job for a farm boy, and James worked hard. He did not say much, so people never really knew what he was thinking. He seemed happy enough in the shop, but in his heart he still wanted to go to sea.

James read every book he could
find about the world's great oceans.
European seamen had been making
maps of the Atlantic Ocean for centuries.
But to James's surprise, the huge Pacific
Ocean was still a mystery. Some geographers
believed that a continent full of people existed
down there. They thought that it "balanced out" all
the land at the top of the world.

When James was 18, he decided to follow his dream. He quit his job at the shop and became an apprentice to John Walker, the owner of a coal-carrying ship at the local port of Whitby. At last he was going to sea—as a cabin boy.

James was big and strong for his age. He also had to be brave, because life on the coal-carrying ships could be tough and dangerous. But James loved every minute of it, and between voyages he read book after book about navigation, the science of keeping ships on course.

John Walker was pleased with James—he was always so calm and reliable. In 1755, he asked James to take command of a coal-carrying ship. But James had other plans. Britain was about to fight a war against France. James joined the navy, and three years later he was crossing the Atlantic Ocean to Canada as ship's master, in charge of navigation on the HMS *Pembroke*.

Britain and France were countries in Europe. But they also ruled over empires made up of lands in other continents. They were fighting now about who should rule Canada.

One dark night in 1759, James had a vital job to do. Ships carrying British soldiers were sailing up Canada's St. Lawrence River. They planned to make a surprise attack on the great French fortress of Quebec. James, the expert navigator, had to map out a safe path for the warships to follow.

This was not easy. The river was wide, fast flowing, and full of rocks. But James calmly guided all the soldiers as far as Quebec. There they rushed ashore, captured the fortress, and then went on to seize all of Canada. James's map of the St. Lawrence River was so good, people were still using it 100 years later.

After the war, James returned to London. He was now 34 years old. Most men of that age were already married. James had been so busy since joining the navy, there had been no time to find a wife.

In 1762, James married a woman named Elizabeth Batts, the daughter of a shopkeeper. They set up house together and soon started a family. But James was hardly ever at home. He spent the next five summers far across the Atlantic Ocean, making detailed maps of Canada's coastlines for the navy.

Then in 1768 James was finally given command of his own vessel—HMS *Endeavour*. It had once been a coal-carrying ship, so James knew exactly how to sail it. His superiors in the navy had decided that he was ready for a very special mission. They were sending him into the vast, little-known Pacific Ocean.

The *Endeavour* set sail from Plymouth on August 26, 1768. The ship was only 105 feet (32 meters) long, but it had to carry 94 men. Some of them were famous scientists. They hoped to sail to the Pacific island of Tahiti. There they would watch the transit of Venus— the movement of the planet Venus across the Sun. That was the official purpose of the expedition.

But James also had some secret orders. He was to search for the Great Southern Continent, which no European had ever found.

It was a difficult voyage for everyone on board. But at last on April 13, 1769, James guided the ship safely into Matavai Bay, Tahiti, in time for the scientists to see the transit of Venus.

Luckily, the native people of Tahiti were very friendly. James enjoyed getting to know their customs. But on July 13, 1769, it was time to move on—into the unknown.

The *Endeavour* sailed west and then south. After three months, a large landmass loomed ahead. It was New Zealand, which had first been seen by Dutch sailors in 1642. Was this a part of the Great Southern Continent? Before James could find out, the local people—the Maoris—made a fierce attack on the *Endeavour*.

Endeavour's crew managed to beat off the Maori war canoes, but they had to stay on constant alert for more attacks. James was unafraid. He took the ship carefully along the coasts, making a map as he went. New Zealand turned out to be made up of two islands.

Heading west again, James found another shore and began to map it. One place was so full of new plants that he called it Botany Bay (botany is the study of plants). His men also spotted some strange hopping animals—kangaroos. James called this wonderful land New South Wales, because it reminded him of Wales in Britain. Later, it would be known as Australia.

It was not easy to sail along Australia's eastern coast. One night, the ship came to a shuddering halt. Terrible cracking noises filled the air. The *Endeavour* had run into the Great Barrier Reef—a ridge of coral just under the water.

Panic broke out as the ship started to sink. But James kept his nerve. Calmly he told his men how to get the ship off the reef. Then they stretched a sail over the hole that was letting in water and sailed to a safe beach to repair it.

When the hole was fixed, the *Endeavour* sailed back home to England. The expedition had lasted for three years. Usually on long voyages many men died of a disease called scurvy, caused by their poor diet. But James had provided healthy food, so his crew was not badly affected.

The voyage had been a huge success. James's report of it made him very famous. Soon New Zealand and Australia were added to the British Empire. But still no one knew for sure if the Great Southern Continent existed.

AUSTRALIA

'Endeavour' ran aground here

NEW ZEALAND

James spent only a year at home with his family. He was promoted again, to commander, and in July 1772 he set out on a second voyage. Again his mission was to find out if there really was a southern continent. This time there were two ships. James commanded the *Resolution*. Tobias Furneaux was in charge of the *Adventure*.

The two ships stopped at Capetown, in southern Africa, and then headed off in search of a southern continent. But the farther south they sailed, the worse the weather became. The crews had never known such cold—even the special warm clothing that James had brought for them did not keep out the chill.

The ships zigzagged around huge icebergs until at last a great sea of ice blocked their path. James now knew the truth. If a southern continent existed, it could only be in these frozen wastes known as the Antarctic—and no people could possibly live there.

The *Resolution* and the *Adventure* went on to map more than 30 new islands in the south Pacific. As they did so, they lost contact with each other.

James and his crew were glad to be back in the warm ocean after almost freezing in their search for the southern continent. One of the most mysterious places they visited was Easter Island. On the grassy slopes of this lonely island, people had carved massive stone heads. Some were more than 30 feet (9 meters) tall. They were so old that the islanders had forgotten what they were for.

When the *Resolution* reached Tahiti, the island's big war fleet put on a show. The Tahitians, like most of the Pacific islanders, were friendly to James's men. But fights sometimes broke out between the islanders and the British sailors.

James looked out for his men and did his best to keep them out of trouble. Some captains in those days were cruel and harsh, but James won his men's loyalty by treating them fairly and kindly. After each voyage some of his crew signed up to sail with him again. They knew he was an unusually good captain.

James had also become an excellent navigator who could use maps, telescopes, and other tools to keep his ship on course. All navigators would find it easier to keep their ships on course in the future, thanks to a brand-new piece of equipment James had brought on this voyage.

This was a chronometer, a sea clock invented by John Harrison. The navy had asked James to test it, and he found that it was very accurate. He called it his "Watch Machine, our never failing guide." It guided James and the *Resolution* back to England in July 1775, where James received a hero's welcome.

Route of Cook's second voyage

James had been ill for a while on the second voyage. He was now 46, which was quite old in those days. And he had spent seven of the last eight years at sea. He believed that his days of adventure were over and planned to spend the rest of his life quietly with his wife and three children.

He was well rewarded for his explorations. He was promoted to captain. The Royal Society—an important club for scientists—made him a member. He was even invited to court, where he was presented to King George III.

Then in 1776, the navy organized a new expedition. Its aim was to see if there was a Northwest Passage, or route from the Pacific to the Atlantic across the top of North America. The earl of Sandwich asked James who he thought should be put in command. James smiled and said he would do the job himself.

In July 1776, the *Resolution* set sail from Plymouth. James called his ship a "Noah's Ark." On board were all sorts of farm animals, to be used for breeding in faraway lands. A second ship, the *Discovery*, was commanded by Charles Clerke.

They went first to New Zealand. James left some rabbits and goats with the Maoris. Then he moved on to Tahiti, and afterward to the Hawaiian Islands, which he had not visited before. The people there greeted him warmly.

In March 1778, James and his crews reached North America's Pacific coast. They followed it northward, making maps as they went and marveling at the Native American peoples with their totem poles and woven bark hats. But finally thick ice barred their way. James had to admit it: There was no Northwest Passage, just as there had been no Great Southern Continent.

The *Resolution* and *Discovery* now had to turn and head back south. James remembered how friendly the people of Hawaii had been. He decided to call there again. The two ships arrived in January 1779.

But this time the Hawaiians were in a different mood. They kept picking quarrels with the crews and stealing their belongings. James was furious. On February 14, he tried to sort out the trouble on his own, at Kealakekua Bay. The Hawaiians were confused. They panicked, surrounded James, and then attacked him. When they stepped away, Captain Cook was dead.

James once wrote that he wanted "to go as far as it is possible for man to go." On his three great voyages of exploration, he went farther than any other man of his time. He helped to complete the map of the world.

Today, there are still places named after him in Alaska, Australia, New Zealand, and Polynesia.

Cook Inlet

PACIFIC OCEAN

Cook Islands

Cook Strait

Mount Cook

Important dates in Captain Cook's life

1728 James Cook born in Marton, England.

1746 James becomes an able seaman on a coal-carrying boat.

1755 James joins the Royal Navy.

1759 James's charts of the St. Lawrence River help win the battle for Quebec.

1762 James marries Elizabeth Batts.

1768–70 On his first major voyage, James visits Tahiti and charts coasts of New Zealand and Australia.

1772–75 On his second voyage, James sights Antarctica and tests the chronometer.

1776–79 James's final voyage, to look for the Northwest Passage across North America.

1779 James killed by angry Hawaiians in Kealakekua Bay.

Index